The
SOLWAY JUNCTION
RAILWAY

by
Stuart Edgar & John M. Sinton

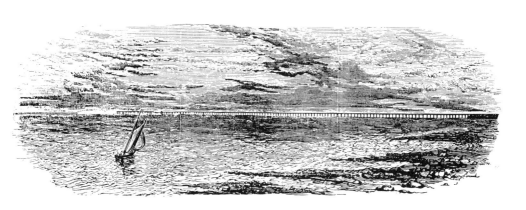

THE OAKWOOD PRESS

© Oakwood Press 1990

ISBN 0 85361 395 8

Typeset by Gem Publishing Company, Brightwell, Wallingford, Oxfordshire.
Printed by Alpha Print, Witney, Oxon.

Acknowledgements

The authors would like to thank the following for their help:

Tullie House Museum, Carlisle
Dumfriesshire Newspapers
Mrs E. Nelson
Mr J. Jackson
Mr N.K. Graham-Barnett
Mr E. Robinson
Mr R. Wright
David & Charles Publishers
Valentines of Dundee
Scottish Record Office
Cumbria Record Office
Dumfries and Galloway Regional Librarian
The Railway Magazine
The Engineer
The Model Railway News

Published by
The OAKWOOD PRESS
P.O.Box 122, Headington, Oxford.

Contents

346.—SOLWAY JUNCTION.

Incorporated by 27 and 28 Vic., cap. 158 (30th June, 1864), to construct a line from the Caledonian, near Kirtlebridge, to the Brayton station of the Maryport and Carlisle, and branches in connection therewith. Length, 25¼ miles. Capital, 320,000*l*. in 10*l*. shares, and 106,600*l*. on loan. Opened for goods traffic on 13th September, 1869.

By 28 and 29 Vic., cap. 186 (29th June, 1865), certain deviations were authorised, power given to use part of the Glasgow and South Western, to make use of the Maryport and Carlisle station, and an agreement with the North British confirmed.

By 29 and 30 Vic., cap. 243 (23rd July, 1866), the company was authorised to raise additional capital to the extent of 60,000*l*. in shares, and 20,000*l*. on loan. Power was also given to the North British and the Glasgow and South Western to subscribe 100,000*l*. each to the Solway Junction.

By 30 and 31 Vic., cap. 116 (15th July, 1867), the company was authorised to construct a junction with the Carlisle and Silloth Bay. Length, 13 chains, and to divide the capital into deferred and preferred shares. The Caledonian was also authorised to guarantee the debenture debt of the Solway Junction, as well as to subscribe a sum not exceeding 100,000*l*. towards the share capital of the undertaking. An extension of time for three years for completion of works was also obtained, while traffic facilities were given to the Furness and London and North Western.

For working agreement between the Caledonian and the Solway Junction, see APPENDIX to present Volume.

CAPITAL.—This account to 30th June showed that 391,430*l*. had been expended, including 46,134*l*. in the past half-year. The estimate of further expenditure was 118,146*l*. for lines in course of construction, the powers and other assets available to meet which were of the same amount.

Meetings in February or March and August or September.

No. of Directors—6; quorum, 3. *Qualification*, 300*l*.

DIRECTORS :

Chairman—ALEX. BROGDEN, Esq., M.P., Ulverstone, and 1, Victoria Street, Westminster, S.W.

Deputy-Chairman—JAMES DEES, Esq., Whitehaven, and Bellingham, Northumberland.

Joseph Fletcher, Esq., Kelton House, Dumfries and Whitehaven.	*Lieut.-Col. Salkeld, Holm Hill, Carlisle.
Hugh Ker, Esq., Annan.	*Andrew Buchanan, Esq., Auchentorlie, Dumbartonshire.

* Directors of the Caledonian Railway Company.

Directors go out of office 1st meeting after opening of the line ; eligible for re-election.

OFFICERS.—Sec., H. F. Tahourdin ; Chief-Eng., James Brunlees, C.E., 5, Victoria Street, Westminster, S.W. ; Solicitors, Messrs. Tahourdin, 1, Victoria Street, Westminster, S.W., and Alexander Downie, Town Clerk, Annan.

Offices—Annan, Dumfriesshire.

Extract from the 1870 Bradshaw's Manual

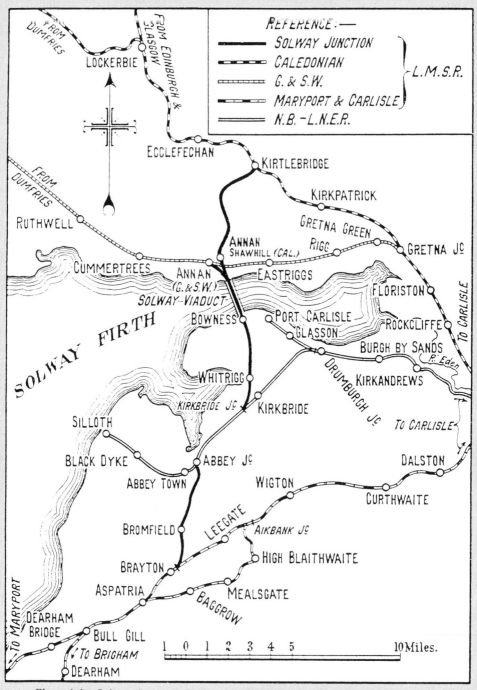

Plan of the Solway Junction Railway and adjoining railways.
Courtesy of The Railway Magazine

Chapter One

The Case for the Railway

In the 1850s the Solway Junction Railway was first planned as a line from the Canonbie coalfield to an intended harbour at Annan, but because of the lack of money and support the scheme never left the drawing board. The railway was planned as a link between the hematite ore mines of Cumberland and the furnaces of Lanarkshire avoiding the long detour via Carlisle.

In 1862 James Brunlees (later Sir James), who was born in Kelso and was a distinguished figure in civil engineering, was asked to come and survey the land for the promoters. He had past experiences with building of bridges across the shifting sands of tidal estuaries, the bridges over the Kent and Leven estuaries in Morecambe Bay (1852–57) establishing his reputation.

During his career he was involved in many works in this country and abroad, including the piers at Southport (the first of its kind), Southend-on-Sea (the largest in the country), work on the Mont Lenis railway, the Mersey railway tunnel and the San Paulo railway. He was also one of the consultants on the proposed Channel tunnel of the 1880s.

Brunlees told the promoters that they were wasting their money because there was already a branch line to Gretna. The making of a parallel line to Annan, apart from the costly scheme of making the river Annan navigable, was not worth the expense. He told them that a group of people in Cumberland were employing him to see if they could make a line and harbour in the Bowness area, and he suggested that the two groups should meet.

Thomas Paterson of Langholm the leader of the Scottish team, and John Musgrave of Whitehaven, the leader of the English team, organized a meeting at Carlisle and a prospectus was drawn up for the Dumfriesshire and Cumberland (Solway Junction) Railway. The title was shortened to the Solway Junction Railway when the Bill was submitted to Parliament for approval.

In May 1864 a Select Committee of the House of Commons commenced the examination of the Dumfriesshire and Cumberland (Solway Junction) Railway Bill. Counsel for the promoters were Mr Mundell and Mr Miller; Counsel for the Glasgow and South Western Railway Company, opposing the Bill, were Mr Burke QC and Mr Granville Somerset.

Mr Mundell opened the case for the promoters. He stated 'that they were an independent company, who had been led to take up the scheme by a sense of the local wants of the district'. There was a large and growing trade in hematite ore from the neighbourhood of

ANNO VICESIMO NONO & TRICESIMO

VICTORIÆ REGINÆ.

✷✷✷*✷*

Cap. ccxliii.

An Act to enable the *Solway Junction* Railway
Company to raise further Capital ; and for other
Purposes. [23d *July* 1866.]

WHEREAS by " The *Solway Junction* Railway Act, 1864," 27 & 28 Vict.
the *Solway Junction* Railway Company (herein called c. clviii.
" the Company ") were incorporated, and authorized to
make and maintain a Railway from the *Caledonian* Railway, near
Kirtlebridge Station, to the *Maryport and Carlisle* Railway, near
Brayton Station, with certain Branch Railways in connexion therewith, in the Counties of *Dumfries* and *Cumberland*, and were further
authorized to raise a Capital of Three hundred and twenty thousand
Pounds in Shares, and to borrow One hundred and six thousand six
hundred Pounds on Mortgage of their Undertaking : And whereas by
" The *Solway Junction* Railway (Deviation) Act, 1865," the Com- 28 & 29 Vict.
pany were authorized to make and maintain certain Railways in c. clxxxvi.
substitution for Portions of their said authorized Line, and the
Company are proceeding to put their said Acts into execution, and
there are no Shares in the Capital of the Company entitled to any
Preference or Priority of Dividend : And whereas the Company are
desirous of constructing the Viaduct for carrying their Railway across
the *Solway Frith* for a double Line of Rails, and for this Purpose
[*Local.*] they

First page of the 1866 Act authorising the company to raise further operating
capital.

Whitehaven, which went to the iron works in Ayrshire, Lanarkshire and Perthshire. At present the traffic to Ayrshire was competed for by the vessels and the Glasgow and South Western (G&SWR). The rest of the Scottish traffic went by the Caledonian, via Carlisle, which was, however, a rather circuitous route. It would be of great advantage to have a more direct line, and that would be afforded by the present project. It was proposed to make a line from Kirtlebridge, on the Caledonian Railway, to Brayton, on the Maryport and Carlisle Railway – a distance of 25 miles – crossing the G&SW by a bridge over a deep cutting, and the Solway Firth by an embankment and viaduct, passing over another small estuary, and sending forth branches to Annan and Annan Waterfoot, to Port Carlisle, and to a point on the Silloth Railway. It was important that the new line should communicate for the purpose of interchanging traffic with both the Caledonian and the G&SW; but if they had to choose between one of the two, they would give the preference to the Caledonian, by means of which alone they could get access to the country where most of the traffic contemplated tended to originate.

It was expected that the aggregate traffic on the new line would yield as much as, in the lowest estimate, £30 per week per mile, and would enable the company to give some handsome dividends. There were other independent local lines in Cumberland which distributed dividends to the amount of 5 and 9 per cent, and in some cases even to a greater amount. The G&SW affected to be very much alarmed lest the Caledonian should get a monopoly of the line, but the fact was they were themselves seeking to get it under their control. The promoters would prefer to work the line themselves, but they sought permissive powers to make traffic arrangements with several companies merely as a provision against contingencies which might arise. Annan would be much benefited by the new railway, as it would place the once flourishing (but of late years rather neglected) port in direct railway communication with important seats of industry and commerce.

The Glasgow and South Western had not behaved correctly to that town. They had declined to make a branch to the waterfoot, and had attempted, in some case, to enforce high charges. For instance, the charge for the carriage of tea from London to Carlisle being 40s. a ton, they asked 30s. additional for taking it from Carlisle to Annan, a distance of 17 miles. The grocers, however, rebelled, carted it themselves at 10s. a ton, and at length the railway company gave way. Mr Mundell hoped the Committee would approve the Bill, which was calculated to confer great public and local advantages. The G&SW were petitioners against the Bill, complaining that the new railway would cross their line in an objectionable manner; but there was no ground for the statement, because the crossing would take place by a bridge over a deep cutting. Further the G&SW alleged that there was a public want for this new line and that if it were to be connected with the Caledonian, and the other traffic arrangements entered into with that railway, traffic which now belonged to the Glasgow and South Western would be directed to the injury of the petitioners. The fact was that by enabling the G&SW to compete on advantageous terms with the sea board the new line would be a decided benefit to them. As to the arrangements with the Caledonian they were purely permissive, and it did not follow that they would be used at all.

Mr Thomas Massicks, Receiver of Whitehaven Harbour, gave evidence as to the imports and exports between that port and Whitehaven. He believed that much of that traffic would go by the new line if it were constructed.

Mr Alexander Downie, town clerk of Annan, said that the Glasgow and South Western having driven off the steamers at that port, then raised their rates. There had been many attempts to procure a railway communicating with the Waterfoot, and the final result had been the present scheme. Before the railways came to Annan, it was an important market town and harbour. It was the shipping place for Dumfries, Lockerbie, and even for points as remote as Moffat, Langholm and Hawick. The largest pork-curing trade in Scotland was established in Annan. There was also a large grain, wood and slate trade, or rather, there had been before the railways diverted the traffic, and at the same time denied Annan a branch to the harbour. Annan was a great manure depot and great quantities of that commodity were sent into Cumberland via Carlisle.

A good many ships were built in Annan, some 1,400 to 1,600 tons burden. Coals for Annan were now shipped from Port Carlisle, discharged at Waterfoot, and then carted into the town. The new line would bring Annan cheap coals, for it would open up the mines within 15 and 18 miles distance. The water traffic to Port Carlisle, exclusive of coals, did not exceed 841 tons a year. The vessels averaged from 20 to 120 tons burden, if this line were opened there would be very little traffic going up to Port Carlisle. At present travellers from Annan to Edinburgh suffered much inconvenience from detention at Gretna. The universal feeling in Annan was in favour of the Bill. It was the same in the surrounding districts. Mr Hugh Kerr, builder of Annan backed Mr Downie's statements as did Mr John Swan, merchant in the same town.

The new company would most probably work their own line. The proposal of the G&SW was that they should have full powers over the new line, and that the promoters should be absolutely debarred

SOLWAY JUNCTION RAILWAY.

— ♦ —

THE CHAIRMAN AND BOARD OF DIRECTORS

REQUEST THE PLEASURE OF

W Wawwright Esqr

COMPANY AT

A DEJEUNER IN ANNAN,

ON TUESDAY, MARCH 28, 1865.

TO CELEBRATE THE CUTTING OF THE FIRST SOD,

BY W. EWART, ESQ.. M.P.

The Favour of an answer, not later than the 20th inst., addressed to the Secretary, 36, King Street, Whitehaven, is particularly requested.

~~~~~~ ~~~~~~

CARDS WILL BE FORWARDED.

~~~~~~ ~~~~~~

ALEX. BROGDEN, *Chairman.*
C. J. TAHOURDIN, *Secretary.*

Invitation to the cutting of the first sod.   *Courtesy PRO Ref. SJR 4/3*

from connecting with any company which might be supposed to be a rival to the Glasgow company. He had no fear that the Committee would concede so imperious and sweeping a demand. The Glasgow and South Western were entitled to all reasonable securities for the full transmission of traffic by the new line, and these the promoters were willing to grant; but it was not right or just that the new and independent company should be put completely under the power of the G&SW. With regard to the doubts which the Admiralty had raised as to the expediency of permitting any interference by railway works of tidal waters, he hoped to be able to show there was no risk or danger or inconvenience in that way.

Sir John Heron Maxwell, owner of the estate of Springkell Dumfries, 7 miles from Annan, was well acquainted with the country from Kirtlebridge to the Solway, and said that there was an unanimous opinion in favour of the line on the part of the proprietors in the district, and also on the part of the public in the towns and elsewhere.

Mr Cook, Secretary and General Manager of the Whitehaven and Furness Railway, of which Lord Lonsdale was Chairman, appeared next. His lordship had authorised him to appear in favour of the Bill. He had been connected with the Whitehaven railways for eight years. In that time 11 blast furnaces had been erected in the district, and two more were in progress. In 1861 the total amount of iron-ore exported from Whitehaven to Scotland was 30,000 tons, and in 1863, 92,000 or an increase of more than three-fold. There also had been an increase of general goods and pig-iron.

Mr Brunlees, Engineer to the new line, said he had also been Engineer to the Morecambe Bay Railway and to somewhat similar works in the north of Ireland. He then stated that the length of the main line from Kirtlebridge to Brayton was 20 miles, 3 furlongs, 3 chains. The steepest gradient was 1 in 80, and the sharpest curve 2 furlongs radius. There was a branch to Annan 2 furlongs, 5 chains in length; another to Annan Waterfoot, 1 mile long; a third went to Port Carlisle, 1 mile 6 furlongs, 2 chains in length; a fourth to the Silloth Railway, 2 furlongs, 3 chains long. The works were all of a very moderate character except that crossing the Solway.

He explained that the waterway of the proposed Solway viaduct would be 80 feet. There were 74 piers, with an interval of a foot between each, and 6 feet for the drawbridge. The drawbridge was later withdrawn from the plans after pressure from local representatives who had commercial interests at Port Carlisle. In return the Solway Junction Railway had to guarantee the rail link between Port Carlisle and Carlisle. The greatest depth of sand in the Solway estuary was 9 feet, and the substratum was clean gravel and hard clay. The solid embankment, which it was proposed to construct, would

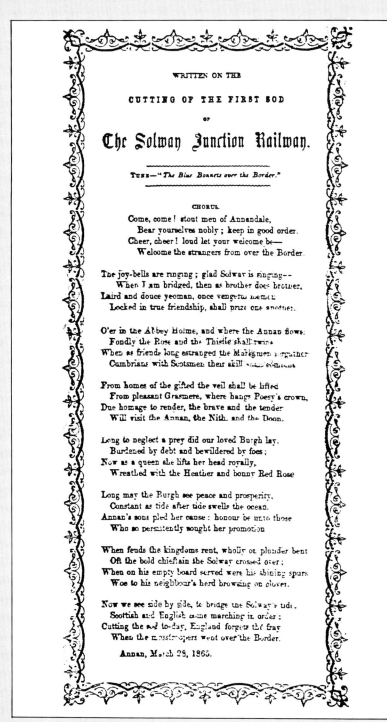

WRITTEN ON THE

CUTTING OF THE FIRST SOD

OF

The Solway Junction Railway.

TUNE—"*The Blue Bonnets over the Border.*"

CHORUS.

Come, come ! stout men of Annandale,
    Bear yourselves nobly ; keep in good order.
Cheer, cheer ! loud let your welcome be—
    Welcome the strangers from over the Border.

The joy-bells are ringing ; glad Solway is singing—
    When I am bridged, then as brother does brother,
Laird and douce yeoman, once vengeful foemen,
    Locked in true friendship, shall prize one another.

O'er in the Abbey Holme, and where the Annan flows,
    Fondly the Rose and the Thistle shall twine
When as friends long estranged the Marksmen forgather
    Cumbrians with Scotsmen their skill will combine

From homes of the gifted the veil shall be lifted
    From pleasant Grasmere, where hangs Poesy's crown,
Due homage to render, the brave and the tender
    Will visit the Annan, the Nith, and the Doon.

Long to neglect a prey did our loved Burgh lay.
    Burdened by debt and bewildered by foes ;
Now as a queen she lifts her head royally,
    Wreathed with the Heather and bonny Red Rose

Long may the Burgh see peace and prosperity,
    Constant as tide after tide swells the ocean.
Annan's sons pled her cause : honour be unto those
    Who so persistently sought her promotion

When feuds the kingdoms rent, wholly on plunder bent
    Oft the bold chieftain the Solway crossed o'er ;
When on his empty board served were his shining spurs
    Woe to his neighbour's herd browsing on clover.

Now we see side by side, to bridge the Solway's tide,
    Scottish and English come marching in order :
Cutting the sod to-day, England forgets the fray
    When the mosstroopers went over the Border.

Annan, March 28, 1865.

The ballad specially written to celebrate the events of 28th March, 1865.

not interfere with the navigation. On the contrary, as far as they could judge from the experience at Morecambe Bay (a very similar case) they believed the channel would probably be deepened and widened thereby. The iron piers on which the viaduct would be carried across the estuary were not more than 15 inches in diameter. There would not be any obstruction to the passing of sailing vessels under the viaduct. The fact was that the tonnage of the most of the vessels that passed that way were very small – not more, on the average, than 50 tons each, and there were, moreover, not many of them. The other works were of an extremely moderate character. The requirements of the Board of Trade as to level crossings, had all been complied with.

The Act for the Solway Junction Railway was incorporated by Parliament on 30th June, 1864, to construct a line from the Caledonian Railway (near Kirtlebridge) to the Brayton Station of the Maryport and Carlisle Railway. Its authorised length was 25¼ miles and a capital of £320,000 in £10 shares allocated.

The first sod was cut at Annan on Tuesday, 28th March, 1865. A medallion was struck to commemorate the event. The inscription on the outer edge reads as follows: 'To commemorate the cutting of the first sod', in the centre, the words 'Solway Junction Railway at Annan by Wm Ewart Esq MP, 28 March 1865'. On the reverse is shown an engine and coach crossing a viaduct and below are two shields, on the left with three lions and on the right, one lion rampant.

A seven verse ballad and chorus (*see previous page*) was also written for the occasion, and was played to the tune 'The Blue Bonnets over the Border'. Were the seven verses to mark the seven members of the committee, which in 1865 proposed the viaduct and railway and after its completion were known by the inhabitants of Annan as the 'Seven Wise Men'?

William Ewart was presented with an inscribed barrow and spade and at 3 o'clock 300 gentlemen adjourned to wine and dine.

Both sides of the commemorative medal described above.   *Author's Collection*

Chapter Two
Building the Line

Sir James Brunlees designed the viaduct and the Wampool river bridge. Both contracts were carried out by Waring Bros and Eckersley. Mr A. McKenon of Brunlees's staff was the Resident Engineer. The viaduct was started in March 1865; at the point where the Solway Firth was crossed the distance from shore to shore was 2,544 yds; of this 1,950 yds consisted of the iron viaduct, averaging 34 ft deep from rails to the sea bed of the Firth, the remainder being sea embankments. The Seafield or north bank was 154 yds long, and 28 ft high at the extreme end, and the south bank 440 yds long, and 29 ft high. The core of these banks was made of clay; the sides were puddled 1 ft deep, and a layer of broken stones embedded in them, and the whole then pitched over with stones from 15 in. to 18 in. deep.

The superstructure was composed of four longitudinal wrought iron girders, each 29 ft 11⅝ in. long and 2 ft 6 in. deep, and having a camber of ½ in. in their length, with expansion joints placed over each of the piers; the platform was formed of Mallet's bucked plates riveted to the girders longitudinally, and to each other by strips transversely. The permanent way was laid on longitudinal timbers, bolted through the girders. The longitudinals were fastened by the usual ties and transoms placed every 10 feet. The rails were held by dogspikes (later rails with chairs were used). There was a boardwalk on the eastern side.

The cast iron columns that carried the girders were placed every 30 ft apart (every 16th being doubled), they were 12 in. in diameter, ⅞ in. thick, and were cast in 9 ft lengths. The meeting faces of the flange joints were turned and securely fixed by eight 1 in. bolts. The bolt holes in the cap for the connection with the girders were 2 in. by 1¾ in.; the excess dimension in the longitudinal line of the girders was to allow for expansion and contraction. The foundation piles for the columns varied in length with the ground. They were hollow, 12 in. in diameter and ⅞ in. thick. They were originally intended to be screwed in, but after many failures, it was decided to reject the screws and use chilled cast points. The bed of the Solway was composed of boulder gravel covered with a variable depth of sand; thus the piles were never screwed down more than 12 ft, the piles generally breaking between 10 ft and 12 ft. The piles were driven by Sisson and White's steam pile driver; a timber dolly was used with a copper ring, between the shoe of the dolly and the pile head. By these 12 to 15 blows were struck per minute with a 25 cwt. monkey, having a 5 ft

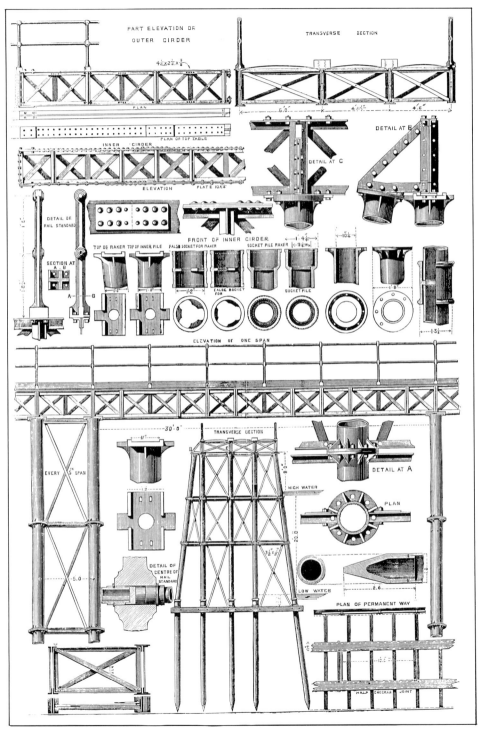

Construction details as recorded in *The Engineer* magazine.

Constructional details of the piles and spans of the viaduct as photographed in 1881. *Author's Collection*

drop. No difficulty was experienced in forcing the piles down 17 ft and 18 ft, although it required from six to ten blows to drive them an inch at this depth. The pile driving was carried out by tidal work, on barges specially constructed; two tides were generally required per pile.

The columns were tied together by means of wrought iron T-sections. In order to provide for future widening, a fifth row of foundation piles was driven, so that with the addition of the outer raking piles the full width could be built with the least possible expense. The total weight of cast iron used in the piles was 2,892 tons, and of wrought iron, 1,807 tons.

The former was specified to be of the best light grey metal, and mixed with such quantity of scrap that a bar 1 in. square, with a length of 4 ft 6 in. between bearings, should not carry less than 700 lb. in the centre before breaking; the wrought iron was of such a quality as to stand the test of 22 tons per square inch.

The whole of the superstructure was erected without scaffolding, the piles being driven at low water, and the columns put into place. Each successive girder was carried over its completed predecessor, and swung into position by means of travelling cranes. The time occupied in erecting one span averaged a day. In all the viaduct had 193 spans. The cost of the viaduct, including sea banks, was reported to be £100,000.

The main work on the viaduct was carried out from a stage which was built at a cost of 6d. per cubic foot, on top of which stood a derrick crane, which was used to lift the piles from the barges.

The contractors used five barges, which were bought at a cost of £250 each. The barges were towed back and forth by a 53 ft long steamer called the *Arabian* which was obtained from the Steam Clyde Shipyard at Glasgow for £575.

The high tides and winds brought flooding, which on several occasions caused some of the barges to sink into the Solway, but on each occasion these were recovered and repaired and brought back into service.

In November 1866 there was a serious accident on the south side of the viaduct, when the middle bearer of the riveting platform broke and a man and boy who were on it at the time fell onto the scaur below. The man was killed and the boy concussed with the inquest returning a verdict of accidental death.

The viaduct took 3½ years to build, and was, in fact, built illegally, the company not realising that the Scottish shore was owned by the Crown Commissioners, and that the English side was part of the Earl of Lonsdale's estate. After a delay, £105 was paid to the Crown Commissioners for the Scottish land. There was an even longer delay on the English side as the Earl and the Crown Commissioners fought over the ownership of the shore and seabed. The viaduct was nine years old before it was finally sanctioned.

The principal work on the English side was the passage over the Bowness Moss. The side near the Firth, for a distance of a mile and a quarter, was unsafe for cattle and horses, except during the driest summers, the moss running in some places to a depth of 50 ft. In order to drain it, however, ditches had to be cut 66 ft apart on either side of the line, together with longitudinal ditches 33 ft apart, along the entire length. By these means the level of the moss was reduced by 4 ft or 5 ft for some distance on either side of the line. The road was formed through the worst parts with two layers of faggots.

The building of the line from Kirkbride Junction to the Wampool river was straightforward with little problem. The piles for the Wampool river bridge were driven 30 ft under the sea bed.

The line from Abbey Junction to Brayton had a slight gradient with no major obstacles. The line in Scotland reached a summit of 296 ft before descending to Kirtlebridge.

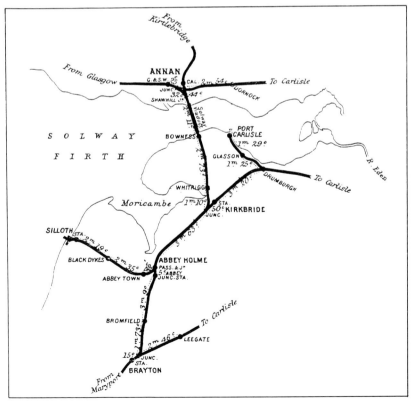

The greater part of the line as shown in the RCH Junction Diagram book (1920).

SOLWAY JUNCTION RAILWAY.

OPENING OF THE LINE

FOR

GOODS AND MINERAL TRAFFIC.

MONDAY. 13th September 1869.

WORKING TIME TABLE.

UP

Mls	Chns		a.m.	a.m.	p.m.
		Leave....Kirtlobridge, ...	6 0	10 3	2 0
2	53	,, Annan......	6 24	10 29	2 24
3	7	,, Shawhill Junction.......	6 15	7 17	2 14
4	47	,, Bowness, ...	6 35	10 40	2 38
6	7	,, Kirkbride Junction......	6 53	10 53	2 53
11	4	,, Abbey Holm Junction,..	7 9	11 14	3 9
21	71	Arrive Brayton Junction,..	7 30	11 38	3 30

DOWN.

			a.m.	noon.	p.m.
		Leave....Brayton Junction,..	8 0	12 0	4 0
11		,, Abbey Holm Junction..	8 11	12 11	4:11
17	7	,, Kirkbride Junction......	8 37	12 37	4 37
18		,, Bowness, ...	8 55	12 55	4 55
19		,, Shawhill Junction,......	9 4	1 4	5 4
20		,, Annan, ...	9 6	1 6	5 6
		,, Kirtlebridge..........	9 30	1 30	5 30

The first timetable for the line unfortunately reproduced from a very poor original. *Author's Collection*

Chapter Three

The Opening of The Solway Junction Railway

According to local newspapers, the first unofficial person to cross the viaduct was a Miss Cottam, daughter of Mr John Cottam a grocer and general dealer at Bowness. When the bridge was nearly finished a foreman promised that the girl should be first to go over as soon as it was completed. He kept his word and on the Sunday morning before it was officially opened he took her across, a little nervous, but very proud to be so privileged.

A train loaded with officials including members of the Board of Trade made a trial trip on 3rd July, 1869 to inspect the line. Two Caledonian Railway locomotives pulled the train. After a few alterations to signals etc., an official application to open the line was submitted.

The line was passed for goods traffic on 1st September, 1869 and for passenger traffic on 8th July, 1870 after allowing time for the viaduct to settle on its foundations. It opened for goods and mineral traffic on Monday 13th September, 1869 without any ceremony. Three goods trains were running each way, leaving Kirtlebridge at 6 am, 10.05 am and 2 pm and leaving Brayton Junction at 8 am, 12 noon and 4 pm, each journey taking 1½ hours for the 21 miles from end to end. Bowness Moss, the softness of which had been the occasion of much anxiety to the contractors, and the cause of considerable delay in the opening of the line, successfully resisted the pressure of the heavy trains, which were composed of wagons filled with iron plates, pig-iron and iron ore.

There had been a service between Kirtlebridge and Annan from 1st October, 1869 which was not shown in public timetables but was advertised in the local press. Passengers first crossed the viaduct on 8th August, 1870 travelling between Kirtlebridge and Bowness; the distance between the two places is approximately eight miles, and the third class fare was 1s. 3d. which was considered rather a high rate. The company were entitled, however, to charge a premium to cross the viaduct.

After crossing the Solway, Bowness was the first passing place and the next was at the junction with the North British at Kirkbride. A station was made at Whitrigg level crossing and opened with the line, but until 1st January, 1873 calls were only made by request or hand signal; from this date it was signalled and a crossing keeper was appointed.

On the same date a station was opened at Bromfield between Abbey Junction and Brayton stations. Until October 1895 the name was always shown in Caledonian Railway time tables as Broomfield.

[36 & 37 Vict.] *The Caledonian Railway (Solway* [**Ch. ccxxviii.**] *Junction Purchase) Act, 1873.*

CHAPTER ccxxviii.

An Act for authorising and carrying into effect the purchase A.D. 1873.
by the Caledonian Railway Company of the portion of the
Solway Junction Railway lying between Annan and Kirtlebridge Junction ; and for other purposes. [5th August 1873.]

WHEREAS an Agreement, dated the twenty-second day of Agreement
March one thousand eight hundred and sixty-seven, was dated 22nd
entered into between the Caledonian Railway Company (herein- March 1867.
after called "the Company") and the Solway Junction Railway
Company (herein-after called "the Solway Company"), whereby it
was, inter alia, provided that the Company should have the option,
at any time during ten years from the said date, of taking and
purchasing, and that the Solway Company should in that case sell
to the Company, that portion of the Solway Company's line lying
north of the Solway between Annan and the Kirtlebridge Junction
of the Caledonian Railway at the cost price thereof, including
interest and all other charges incidental to that portion of the line
up to the time of opening thereof ; and that the said two Companies
(herein-after called "the two Companies") should concur in a joint
application to Parliament for authority for the said purchase and
sale :

And whereas the said agreement was sanctioned and confirmed
by " The Caledonian Railway (Abandonment, &c.) Act, 1869 :"

And whereas the Company resolved to avail themselves of the
said option, and intimated such resolution to the Solway Company
in the month of February one thousand eight hundred and seventy-
two ; and it is expedient that the said purchase and sale should be
authorised and carried into effect, and that the Company should be
empowered to raise money for enabling them to pay the purchase
money :

And whereas the Annan and Kirtlebridge line, as in the third
section of this Act defined, is the subject agreed to be so purchased
and sold ; and it has been agreed between the two companies that

[*Local.—228.*]

The first page of the authorisation for the Caledonian Railway to purchase
part of the Solway Junction Railway in 1873.

From 1st July, 1904 Abbeyholme station on the North British line was used in lieu of Abbey Junction.

The train service ran each week day with no service on Sundays. The mid-morning train was 'mixed' from Kirtlebridge to Bowness; here the coaches were detached, and the freight portion continued to Brayton. A locomotive which was known as the 'empty engine' came from Kirtlebridge in the afternoon to work the coaches back. On Fridays during autumn, a third class coach was attached to the empty train to provide a passenger service for the farmers returning to Bowness from the Annan market. One way or another this involved tender-first working with a passenger train over the viaduct which had been ruled out by the inspecting officer when the line was opened.

Other passenger trains ran locally from Kirtlebridge to Annan. This service allowed passengers to connect with the main line trains denied to the Solway line stations, which irritated the Solway's Board. Other freight trains crossed the viaduct; the 7.50 am southbound Caledonian mineral train from Carstairs was extended to Bowness, returning at 1.15 pm. Other southbound passenger trains conveyed 'through' goods wagons, running 'mixed', and the last northbound passenger train took livestock from Annan and cleared the Shawhill branch of all goods traffic. The first up goods train called specially at Bowness and Whitrigg only to attach livestock. These trains passed in the early hours, the first train leaving between 3.15 and 5.30 am. As can be expected, talks of a toll charge figured frequently on the agenda of the Solway Board meetings.

The Caledonian Railway Company had put forward most of the money for the construction of the Railway. At first the line was profitable with the ore trains for Lanarkshire passing over the line. But in the mid-1870s the ore traffic began to decline due to the cheaper imports of Spanish ore, and the Solway Junction Railway increasingly experienced financial difficulties as its capital was swallowed up. Revenue decreased from £2,038 in 1874 to a loss of £574 in 1880 to service a capital of £360,000. The company Secretary was at one point unable to bank any cash for fear of seizure by creditors.

In 1873 the Caledonian bought the Scottish section from Kirtlebridge to Annan for the sum of £84,000 in the Solway Junction Purchase Act of 5th August, 1873, and the line was transferred on 9th September, 1873. The remainder of the Solway Junction Railway was transferred to the Caledonian by the Transfer Act of 6th July, 1895, together with all rights and privileges.

CHAPTER cxxxii.

An Act to transfer the Solway Junction Railway to the
Caledonian Railway Company and for other purposes.   A.D. 1895.

[6th July 1895.]

WHEREAS by the Solway Junction Railway Act 1864 the   27 & 28 Vict.
Solway Junction Railway Company (herein-after called " the   c. clviii.
Company ") were incorporated and authorised to make and maintain
railways in the counties of Dumfries and Cumberland :

And whereas by the Solway Junction Railway (Deviation) Act   28 & 29 Vict.
1865 the Company were authorised to make and maintain other   c. clxxxvi.
railways in substitution for portions of the railway authorised by
the Solway Junction Railway Act 1864 :

And whereas by the before-mentioned and various other Acts
of Parliament certain powers rights and privileges have been
conferred on the Company and provisions made in relation to their
undertaking :

And whereas the Company completed and opened their railways
for traffic and the said railways have since the opening thereof been
worked by the Caledonian Railway Company (herein-after called
" the Caledonian Company ") under heads of agreement scheduled
to and confirmed by the Caledonian Railway (Abandonment &c.)   32 & 33 Vict.
Act 1869 and under an agreement scheduled to and confirmed by   c. cxxvi.
the Caledonian Railway (Additional Powers) Act 1890 :   53 & 54 Vict.
                                                          c. cxxxi.
And whereas under the powers in that behalf contained in the   36 & 37 Vict.
Caledonian Railway (Solway Junction Purchase) Act 1873 the   c. ccxxviii.
Caledonian Company purchased and acquired that portion of the
Company's line situate between Annan Station and the junction
of the Company's line with the Caledonian Railway at Kirtlebridge
Station :

And whereas the capital of the Company at present issued
consists of—

(A) Thirty thousand pounds three and a half per cent. first
   debenture stock ;

[*Price* 1s. 3d.]

The first page of the Act authorising the Caledonian Railway to purchase the
whole of the Solway Junction Railway.

The 10.47 am from Kirtlebridge seen here arriving at Annan (Shawhill) with CR 4–4–0T No. 15027 in charge of its one coach service in the 1930s.

Courtesy J.J. Cunningham

RAILWAY TIME-TABLE FOR JULY, 1889.

Solway Junction Railway.

	a.m.	a.m.	a.m.	p.m.	p.m.
GLASGOW (Central)..leave	..	6 40	10 35	2 15	4 30
EDINBURGH (Prin. St.),,	..	6 50	10 35	2 20	4 20
KIRTLEBRIDGE....arrive	6 15	10 25	1 20	5 5	7 35
ANNAN .... { arrive leave	6 27	10 37	1 31	5 17	7 50
	6 28	10 38	1 32	5 18	7 53
BOWNESS........ ,,	6 36	10 46	1 40	5 26	8 8
WHITRIGG .... ,,	a	a	a	a	a
ABBEY JUNCTION arrive	6 56	11 6	1 58	5 46	8 35
ABBEY JUNCTION ..leave	10 31	..	2 41	7 13	9 0
SILLOTH ....arrive	10 50	..	3 0	7 30	9 20
SILLOTH ....leave	..	8 0	11 30	4 30	8 0
ABBEY JUNCTION ..arrive	..	8 14	11 46	4 46	8 16
ABBEY JUNCTION leave	6 57	11 7	1 59	5 47	8 36
BROOMFIELD .... ,,	a	a	a	a	a
BRAYTON ....arrive	7 10	11 20	2 10	6 0	8 48
MARYPORT .... ,,	7 50	12 0	2 42	6 35	9 20
COCKERMOUTH .... ,,	8 2	12 25	2 55	6 48	10 20
WHITEHAVEN .... ,,	8 35	12 40	3 0	7 5	10 0

	a.m.	a.m.	a.m.	p.m.	p.m	p.m
WHITEHAVEN ....leave	..	6 30	10 20	1 10	5 15	6 45
COCKERMOUTH .... ,,	..	..	10 88	1*27	5 35	7 0
MARYPORT .... ,,	7 5	11 0	1 48	6 0	7 28
BRAYTON .... ,,	8 15	11 45	2 27	6 25	9 0
BROOMFIELD .... ,,	a	a	a	a	a
ABBEY JUNCTION arrive	..	8 28	11 58	2 40	6 37	9 13
ABBEY JUNCTION ..leave	..	10 31	..	2 41	7 3	..
SILLOTH ....arrive	..	10 50	..	3 0	7 20	..
SILLOTH ....leave	..	8 0	11 30	..	4 0	8 0
ABBEY JUNCTION ..arrive	..	8 14	11 46	..	4 16	8 16
ABBEY JUNCTION leave	..	8 29	11 59	2 41	6 38	9 14
WHITRIGG .... ,,	a	a	a	a	a	a
BOWNESS .... ,,	..	8 54	12 23	3 10	7 0	9 34
ANNAN .... { arrive leave	..	9 1	12 30	3 18	7 7	9 40
	7 25	9 5	12 50	3 20	7 8	..
KIRTLEBRIDGE ..arrive	7 40	9 20	1 5	3 35	7 20	..
EDINBURGH (Prin. St.),,	11 18	12 27	4 15	7 30	10 5	..
GLASGOW (Central).. ,,	11 6	12 37	4 20	7 25	10 18	..

a Trains will only call at Whitrigg and Broomfield to take up and set down Passengers. * Mondays only. † Saturdays only.

Timetable for July 1889, as it appeared in the local press.

KIRTLEBRIDGE, ANNAN, and BRAYTON.—Caledonian.

Miles from Kirtlebdg	Up.	Week Days.						Miles	Down.	Week Days.					
		mrn	mrn	non	aft	aft	aft			mrn	mrn	mrn	aft	aft	aft
	843 GLASGOW (Cen.) dp.		6 35	12 0	..	2 5	4 30	..		Brayton ....dep.	..	7 50	11 30	2 27	..	6 30
	843 EDINBURGH ,,		6 45	12 0	..	2 ..	4 15	..	2	Bromfield .... ,,	..	7 57	11 37	2 34	..	8 35
5¼	Kirtlebridge ....dep.	7 45	10 35	2 35	4 50	5	5 7	45	5¾	Abbey Junction 796 ,,	..	8 18	11 46	2 40	..	6 41
	Annan 820, 821 ,,	8 5	11 50	2 45	5	25	15	7 8 58	10¼	Whitrigg .... ,,	..	8 33	12 10	..	..	6 50
8	Bowness............ ,,	8 13	11 35	2 47	5	9	..	8 8 4	13	Bowness............ ,,	..	8 42	12 25	..	..	6 57
11	Whitrigg............ ,,	8 21	11 50	2 54	5 17	..	..		15¾	Annan 820, 821 { 843	6 15	9 10	12 50	..	4 17	7 5
16	Abbey Junction 796 ,,	8 42	12 15	..	5 29	..	..		21¼	Kirtlebridge 836, arr.	6 26	9 22	1 5	..	3 10	7 15
19¼	Bromfield............ ,,	8 49	12 23	..	5 35	..	..		105¾	836 EDINBURGH * arr.	9 30	12 18	4 5	..	5 45	10 53
21¼	Brayton 504 .... arr.	8 55	12 30	..	5 40	..	..		107	836 GLASGOW (Cen.) ,,	9 30	12 35	4 10	..	5 55	11 0

leaves at 6 40 mrn. on Mondays.   s Saturdays only.   * Princes Street.

Bradshaw's timetable for 1908.

KIRTLEBRIDGE, ANNAN, and BRAYTON.—Caledonian.

Miles from Kirtlebridg	Up.	Week Days only.						Miles	Down.	Week Days only.						
	Central Station.	mrn	mrn	non	mrn	aft	aft			mrn	mrn	mrn	aft	aft	aft	aft
	897 GLASGOW ....dep.	..	6 25	..	10 35	2	3 4 30	..		Brayton ....dep.	..	7 40	11 30	..	2	..	6 30
	897 EDINBURGH * ,,	..	6 30	..	10 15	9	4 15	..	2	Bromfield .... ,,	..	7 47	11 37		2	45	5 16
5¼	Kirtlebridge........dep.	7 45	10 38	..	1 57	5	8 7 50	..	5¾	Abbey Junction { arr. 861 { dep.	..	7 54	11 43		2	51	5 22
	Annan 876, 877 { arr. { dep.	7 56	10 53	..	2 7	5 18	8 2	..			..	8 13	11 46		2	..	5 27
8	Bowness............ ,,	8 10	..	11 30	..	5 20	..	..	10¼	Whitrigg .... ,,	..	8 28	12 10		2	..	5 43
11	Whitrigg............ ,,	8 18	..	11 40	..	5 27	..	..	13	Bowness............ ,,	..	8 37	12 25		..	..	5 51 6a35
16	Abbey Junction { arr. { dep. 861	8 30	..	11 49	..	5 35	..	..	15¾	Annan 876, 877 { arr. { dep.	..	8 45	12 33	..	2	7 7	9 43
		8 42	..	12 8	..	5 45	..	..			6 25	9 0	12 50	2 13	3	..	6 5 6 55
19¼	Bromfield............ ,,	8 49	..	12 28	..	5 53	..	..	21¼	Kirtlebridge 890 arr.	6 29	9 10	1 2	3 4	5	..	6 15 7 10
21¼	Brayton 565 ....arr.	8 55	..	12 45	..	5 58	..	..	105¾	890 EDINBURGH * arr.	9 30	12 30	4 20	5 55	55	..	9 5 11 5
									107	890 GLASGOW (Cen.) ,,	9 32	12 35	4 20	6 0	6	..	9 10 11 5

a Thursdays and Saturdays.   * Princes Street.

Bradshaw's timetable for 1914.

KIRTLEBRIDGE, and ANNAN.—Caledonian.

Mls. from Kirtlebrg.	Up.	Week Days only.							Miles	Down.	Week Days only.			
		mrn	mrn	mrn		aft	aft	aft			mrn	aft	aft	aft
	831 GLASGOW (C.) dep.	..	6 5	10 25		12 45	1 40	4 10			Annan ....dep.	8 20	12 40	3 10	6 25
	831 EDINBURGH † ,,	..	6 30	10 10		12 53	1 30	4 10	5¼	Kirtlebridge 824 arr.	8 32	12 52	3 22	6 37
	Kirtlebridge......dep.	7 45	10 50	2 0		4 35	4 45	7 22	85¾	824 EDINBURGH † arr.	12 45	2 20	0	9 15
5¼	Annan 812, 813... arr.	8 0	11 5	2 12		4 50	5 0	7 34	91¼	824 GLASGOW (Cen.) ,,	12 43	2 20	6 9	17

A Arrives at 12 31 aft. on Saturdays.   B Arrives at 9 23 aft. on Saturdays.   † Princes Street.   ‡ Station for Eaglesfield.

Bradshaw's timetable for the northern portion of the line after closure of the viaduct, 1922.

Kirtlebridge and Annan.

	a.m.	a.m.	a.m.	p.m.	p.m.	Sats. only. p.m.	Ex. Sats. p.m.
Glasgow (Central) ..... depart		6 45	10 25	1 45p	1 40	4 10	
Edinburgh (Princes Street) ... ,,		6 30	10 10	12 53	1 30	4 10	
Kirtlebridge ....depart	7 45		10 35	4 30	4 45	7 22	
Annan ....arrive	8 0	10 50	1 57	4 45	5 0	7 34	

	a.m.	a.m.	p.m.	p.m.	p.m.
Annan ....depart	8 20	12 28	3 20	6 0	9 21
Kirtlebridge ....arrive	8 32	9 12	12 52	3 22	6 37
Edinburgh (Princes Street) ..arrive		12 45	3 20	6 0	9 20
Glasgow (Central) ..... ,,		12 3	3 20	6 5	9 20

LMS timetable for July 1923.

Chapter Four

Disaster Strikes!

Six years after the opening, the first trouble hit the viaduct. During an extra severe winter some of the hollow pillars were cracked by frost, but the damage was quickly repaired by drilling holes in the columns which allowed the water to escape when the tide dropped. During its life span the viaduct was damaged by frost and gales on 30 occasions.

The Solway coast and the Firth have experienced many 'arctic' winters, but the one which is still referred to is the great freeze of 1880/81, when the Rivers Eden and Esk froze in the upper reaches of the Firth. At the end of the second week of January vertical cracks were reported in two of the piers and a number of braces; repair work was quickly carried out under extremely cold conditions.

The Caledonian method of examining the viaduct was to send a man across first thing in the morning and the last thing at night to give a visual inspection of the structure. His reward for doing so was to have his 'bait' (refreshments) in an observation post (wooden hut) constructed on the viaduct. The railway watchman and the local inhabitants could just keep warm and wait for the thaw. At last the thaw set in, and during the week leading up to Saturday 29th January, 1881 the ice began to melt. At first small pieces of ice were carried down the Solway on the fast moving tides, which were common to this estuary, but by the end of the week great chunks of ice were reported by the locals as being as large as 27 yds square and 6 ft thick. When these large blocks of ice forced their way into and between the vertical pillars the whole structure vibrated and the sound was similar to artillery fire. At nine o'clock when the last train passed over the viaduct an inspector made a routine check. Due to the damage earlier in the week, it was decided to place four watchmen on night duty who kept watch from their little cabin on the viaduct.

At 10.30 pm as the ebb tide started running, icebergs again began to bombard the structure and the current was said to be running at between 10 and 15 miles per hour. The four watchmen sat in their cabin listening to the frightening sounds echoing to the north and south of them. The sounds grew steadily worse as the night went on and by the early hours of the morning the foreman had no choice but to abandon their task.

The next day local people gathered on each shore to stare at the viaduct falling to pieces. As each portion of steel fell against the next, sparks lit up the area; it must have been an unforgettable sight. For a ¼ mile from Bowness embankment there was little damage; beyond that there were gaps where whole piers had been demolished, leav-

Two views showing the enormous damage to the viaduct caused by ice forming during the month of January 1881.   *Courtesy Scottish Record Office*

The 'power of the ice' can be seen in this view, the twisted metalwork a clear demonstration of nature's power! *Courtesy Scottish Record Office*

The enormous gap in the structure is apparent, although the west-side rail remains intact even including its fish plates. *Courtesy Scottish Record Office*

ing many girders unsupported. Fallen girders, layers of ice up to 10 feet high resting against the piers, all this told its own story.

During the next few days the tides continued to pull continuous flows of ice down the Firth. The damage grew worse and the work of the spring tide was shrouded in a blanket of fog which covered the entire estuary. Not until the Wednesday did the fog lift to enable the Engineers to see the full extent of the damage. Piers 70–73 with their superstructure were gone, but the west side rail, complete with fish plates and chairs remained, suspended over a 50 yard gap (the 'Scotch gap'). Piers 96–124, with their superstructure had fallen, creating a 300 yard gap (the 'Cumberland gap'). Twelve other piers had fallen leaving girders suspended; in the remaining piers girders lay on the east of the fallen piers.

The total damage to the viaduct was such that, out of its 193 piers, 45 piers and 37 girders had collapsed. The majority of this damage was around the centre and the Scottish side of the viaduct.

By the end of the week the Solway was clear of ice and the tides ran freely to and fro' past the broken structure. Fortunately there had been no loss of life.

Major Marindin, the inspecting officer for the Board of Trade began his Inquiry on 21st February at the Queensberry Arms Hotel at Annan. He was quick to report that because of the thickness of ice and size of the floes, and with no wind to break them up, it was not surprising that the cast iron columns could not withstand the shock. In one small brief reference to the Tay Bridge, he said that cast iron pipes were equally unreliable when exposed to heavy transverse strain from wind, and that this method of construction should be avoided in estuaries where the climate was subject to sudden changes in temperature and blows from floating ice.

The major stated that there was some evidence that the close proximity of the piers had contributed to their destruction, and he concluded that if the outer columns (rakers) had been of sufficient strength the viaduct would not have fallen. He had no objection to the rebuilding of the viaduct but he recommended that ice fenders or wrought iron rakers of adequate strength be used, strong wooden rail guards to prevent derailment should be provided and consideration should be given to increasing the width of the centre spans. On the whole everyone emerged without criticism, which was a relief to Brunlees. All that remained was to find the money and motivation to rebuild the structure.

Traffic arrangements were made by the Caledonian's Carlisle agent who arranged with the M&C to exchange all Solway traffic at Carlisle. (This was done without consulting the Caley's General Manager

James Smithells.) The following day the North British Railway offered to work all traffic via Kirkbride and Carlisle. The Caley also made an offer to the Solway company to take their traffic which would relieve the latter of the NB's toll between Abbeytown and Kirkbride. The Caley would work the Abbey–Brayton traffic including the NBR coke trains and a number of trains between Abbeytown and Bowness. The M&C, however, had its own ideas, and, in turn, made a counter-offer which would give it a percentage of the revenue made from the diverted traffic to the Solway.

After many offers and counter-offers the M&C proposal was accepted. The NB were far from happy as the delays caused by the M&C's lack of locomotives led to a fall in demand, and their coke traffic dropped considerably over the next two years.

In the following year authority was obtained from Parliament for the raising of £30,000 to be devoted to repairing and strengthening the viaduct. Once the long task of repair had begun, the first work to be carried out was the erection of protection booms which was done by Messrs Cowans & Sheldon, the Carlisle crane builders. The main work of repairing the viaduct was supervised by Mr John Brown, the Solway's Resident Engineer.

Ironically the company made more money out of diverting the traffic than it would have done had the viaduct been in use. The line was not reopened throughout until 1st May, 1884.

Work on repairing the viaduct after the storm; cranes are poised on either side. *J. Jackson*

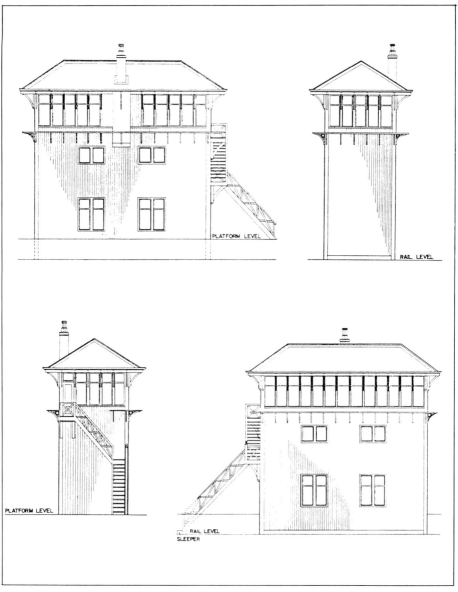

Details of Kirtlebridge's tall signal cabin, controlling the junction with the
Solway Junction Railway.   *Courtesy, Model Railway News*

THIS NEXT SECTION PORTRAYS A TRIP ALONG THE LINE (from north to south) using photographs and plans.

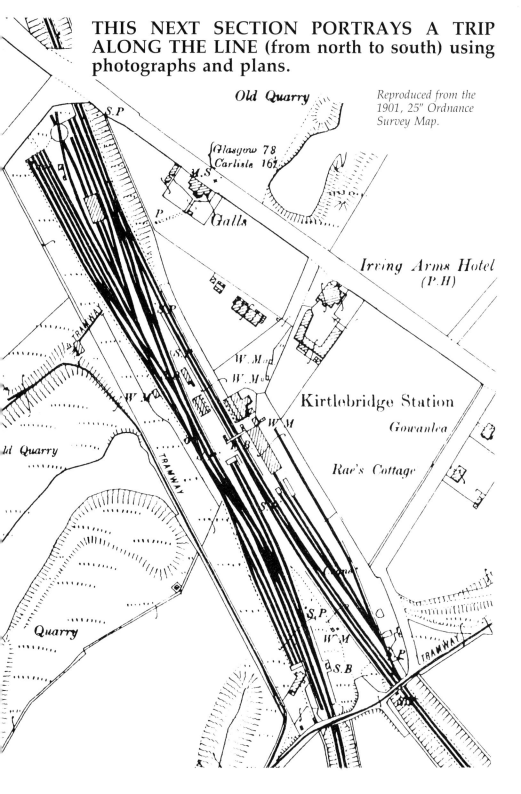

Reproduced from the 1901, 25" Ordnance Survey Map.

Old Quarry

S.P

Glasgow 78
Carlisle 16½

M.S

P.

Galls

Irving Arms Hotel
(P.H)

W.M

W.M

W.M

Kirtlebridge Station

Gowanlea

Rae's Cottage

TRAMWAY

W M

ld Quarry

W M

S.B

S.P

Quarry

S.P

W.M

S.B

TRAMWAY

The locomotive shed at Kirtlebridge as seen in June 1936. The station with its very tall signal box can be seen on the left.   *W.A. Camwell*

A fine view of Kirtlebridge station and close-up of the signal box (*see page 30*).
Courtesy David and Charles

Another view of Caledonian 4–4–0T No. 15027 with its short train, seen here at Annan (Shawhill) in 1930s. *Courtesy J.J. Cunningham*

Annan (Shawhill) looking north. Note the grounded coach body on the left and also the milk churns awaiting collection. *Courtesy David and Charles*

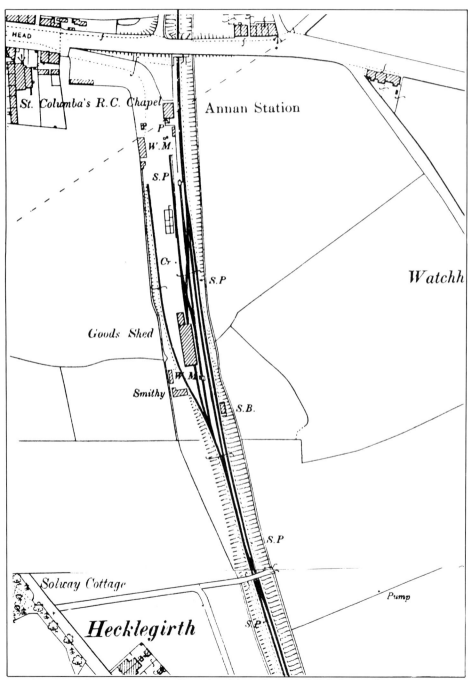

Annan station.   *Reproduced from the 1901, 25" Ordnance Survey Map*

A mixed train leaving Annan (Shawhill) on last day of passenger service with a LMS (former Caledonian) 4–4–0 No. 14463 in charge.

Courtesy J.J. Cunningham

A final view in the 1930's of Annan (Shawhill) looking south showing a CR 4–4–0T on a Kirtlebridge–Annan train.   *Courtesy David and Charles*

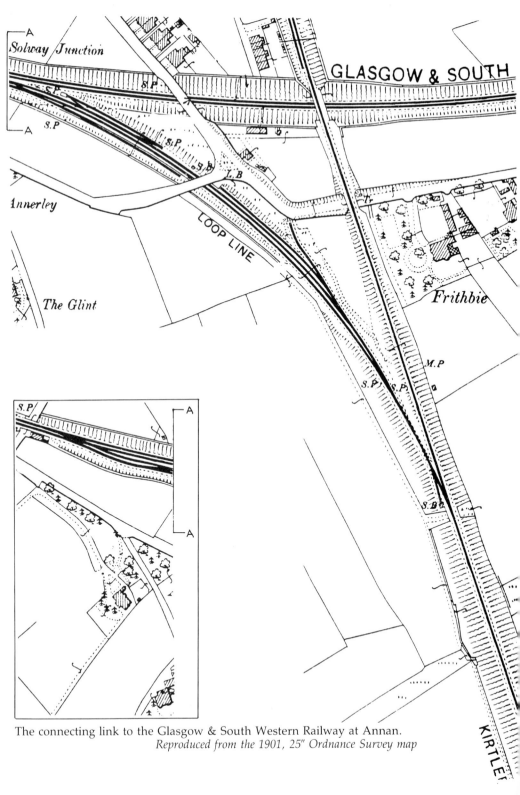

The connecting link to the Glasgow & South Western Railway at Annan.
Reproduced from the 1901, 25" Ordnance Survey map

LMS (ex-CR) 4–4–0 No. 14454 seen here on an empty stock, cattle and sheep special, standing on the connection between Shawhill Junction and G&SW Junction.   *Courtesy David and Charles*

An early postcard view of the viaduct seen from the Annan side of the estuary.   *Author's Collection*

SOLWAY VIADUCT, ANNAN.   56237 (JV)

A view looking northwards in 1929 from Bowness station overbridge, over the Solway viaduct spanning the Solway Firth. The lower picture shows the overbridge and Bowness station looking south.

Courtesy L.G.R.P. Collection, David and Charles

Entitled 'Evening on the Solway, Bowness on Solway', this postcard illustrates the considerable length and fragile construction of the Solway viaduct. *Author's Collection*

A good detailed view of the construction of the decking and showing the method of rail fixing on the viaduct. *Author's Collection*

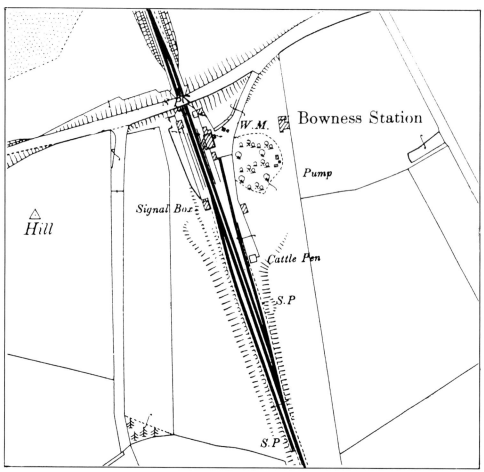

Bowness station.   *Reproduced from the 1901, 25" Ordnance Survey map*

Playing on the sand near the Solway viaduct.   *Author's Collection*

Bowness station looking north in 1929.
L.G.R.P. Collection, courtesy David and Charles

Bowness station looking south; photographed in 1913 with locals and station staff posing for the occasion. *Tullie House Museum Collection*

The rail bridge over the River Wampool (between Whitrigg and Kirkbridge Junction, photographed in 1930 (*see opposite for plan*).   *G.J. Aston*

Bowness station buildings, now a private dwelling as photographed in May 1988.   *Author's Collection*

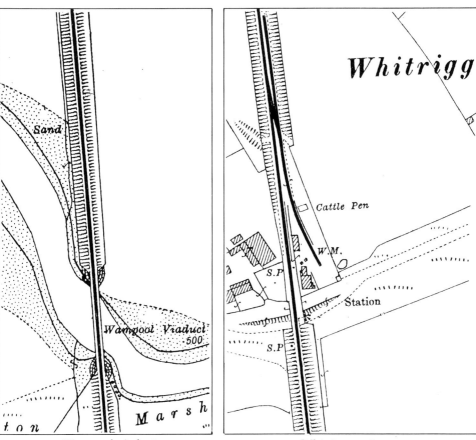

Wampool viaduct.   Whitrigg station.
Reproduced from the 1901, 25" Ordnance Survey map.

The diminutive Whitrigg station looking north.   *G.J. Aston*

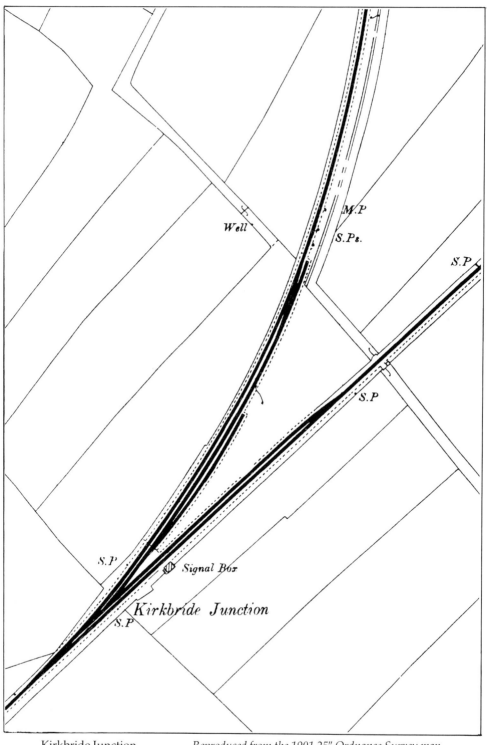

Kirkbride Junction.   *Reproduced from the 1901 25″ Ordnance Survey map.*

Kirkbride Junction, looking south in 1929.
L.G.R.P. Collection, courtesy David and Charles

All that remains of Abbey Junction station in May 1988. *Author*

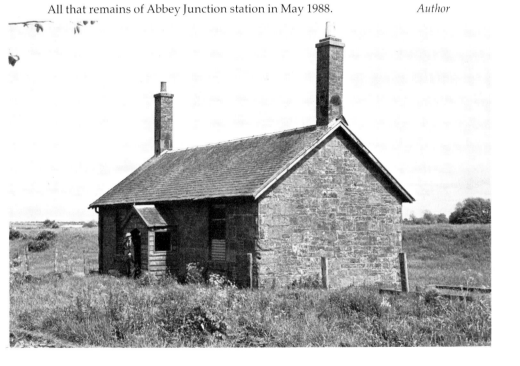

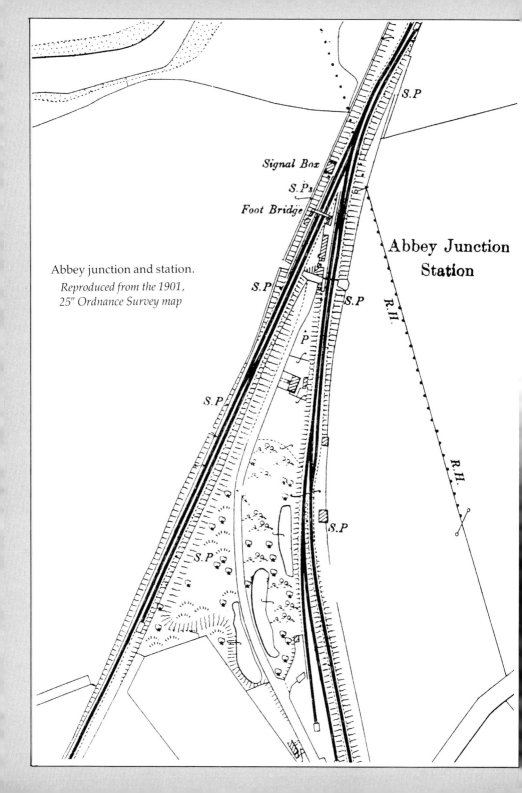

Abbey junction and station.

Reproduced from the 1901, 25" Ordnance Survey map

Signal Box

S.Ps

Foot Bridge

S.P

S.P

S.P

P.

S.P

S.P

S.P

S.P

S.P

Abbey Junction Station

R.H.

R.H.

Waiting at Abbey Station junction in 1929, this LMS (ex-LNWR) 0–6–0 No. 8414 is preparing to return to Maryport.
L.G.R.P. Collection, courtesy David and Charles

Abbey Junction photographed from the North British Railway line in 1929, looking north. The Abbey station can be seen with wagons standing on the adjacent sidings. *L.G.R.P. Collection, David and Charles*

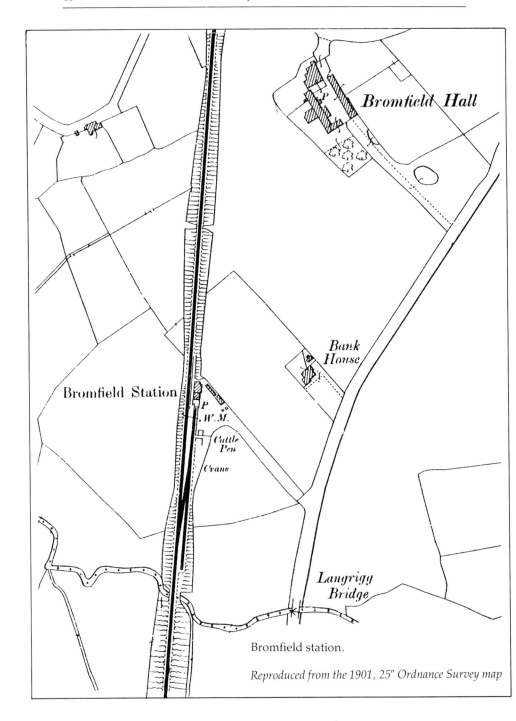

Bromfield station.

Reproduced from the 1901, 25" Ordnance Survey map

The station building at Bromfield photographed in 1929.
L.G.R.P. Collection, courtesy David and Charles

Manchester South Junction and Altrincham Joint Railway coaches standing in Brayton sidings. *Author's Collection*

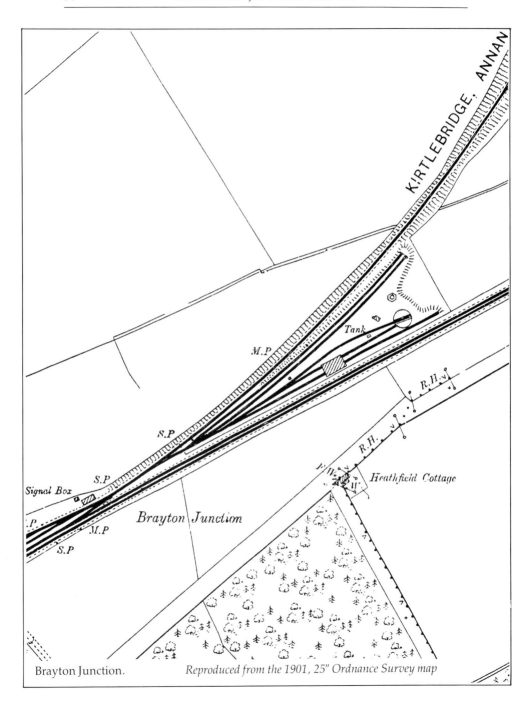

Brayton Junction.   *Reproduced from the 1901, 25" Ordnance Survey map*

Brayton Junction. The Solway Junction Railway can be seen curving off to the left whilst the main Maryport to Carlisle line runs to the right.

Author's Collection

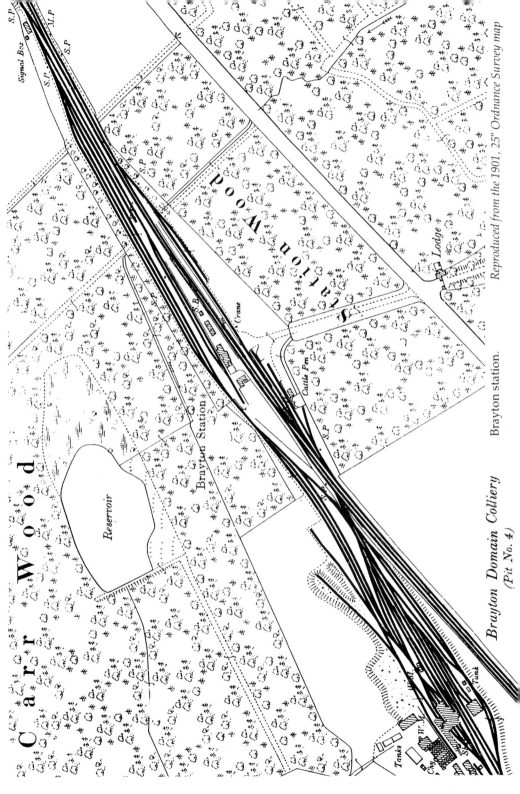

Brayton station.

Reproduced from the 1901, 25″ Ordnance Survey map

Chapter Five

Closure and Demolition of the Solway Viaduct

During a special examination made in 1914 it was found that viaduct repairs amounting to around £15,500 would be required during the next three years, but the outbreak of war stopped all such work, except for limited maintenance as from 1st February, 1915.

By May 1915 a speed restriction of 10 mph had been placed on the bridge, later further reduced to 5 or 8 mph; in the event of strong winds blowing no train was to pass until the 'bridge-gang' had walked across and declared all was well.

However, World War I gave the viaduct a fresh lease of life. Pig iron was urgently required and the Caledonian engineers, foreseeing this, had ordered special lightweight locomotives for the route. These engines though small, could pull 20 to 25 loaded wagons and the one carriage which was all that was needed for the passenger service at that time.

There was a miners' strike in May 1921, and on 20th May the Caledonian Railway and the other Scottish lines cut their already pruned services more drastically. The SJR service (one return mixed train daily) was stopped, but according to locals was resumed on 30th May as one mixed train on Tuesdays and Saturdays only. Early in August 1921, an examination of the viaduct revealed that repairs costing £70,000 were needed.

On 31st August, 1921 after the last train had crossed the bridge the viaduct was closed to traffic, as it was no longer considered safe for trains to cross, and the management were unable to meet the high costs of repair. The lines between Annan and Kirtlebridge, and Brayton and Abbey Junction continued to be used until a much later date for both passenger and freight traffic; indeed the latter section was used in the Summer season in connection with excursions from such points as Workington and Maryport to Silloth.

The closure of the viaduct to rail traffic in 1921, however, did not mean the end of its use, as many a Scottish Border Romeo slipped secretly across the Solway viaduct to keep rendezvous with his fair English Juliet! Furthermore, many Scots denied licensed hospitality in those days on the Sabbath would daringly get round the law by walking across the viaduct, their aim being to enjoy the jovial thirst-quenching atmosphere of an English Inn. Even after the viaduct was declared dangerous, these 'excursions' continued along the line on which no trains ran.

After the closing of the railway as a through route, the LNWR and

Miss Bury (and her friend) standing on the viaduct in 1931.   *E. Nelson*

Reverend Bury and Miss Bury standing on the end of the embankment at Bowness after demolition of the viaduct.   *E. Nelson*

Caledonian Railway merged in 1923 to form the LMS Railway. When the LMS refused to repair the bridge, an approach was made to the Ministry of Transport to have the structure altered to a roadway. But the Ministry of Transport found it would cost at least £91,500 to carry out the work required and the structure would still have had a doubtful life-span. So an abandonment procedure was prepared and was authorised to become effective in 1933.

In 1934 a Glasgow company, Messrs Arnott Young & Co. Ltd bought the bridge and with approval started dismantling it in May 1934. About half of the columns were in reasonable condition and went to East Wemyss pits and Scottish oil works for further service as water pipes. Some of the other pipes went as scrap to Darlington and Motherwell for smelting, while the rest was shipped to Japan to be put in use for armaments in the Sino–Japanese war. Although in the viaduct's 65 years' life, 30 cases of damage had been recorded, when the demolishers got to work they found the structure so firm they could only get it apart by blasting! Consequently close liason was maintained between the demolishers and the local Solway fishermen with regards to the state of the tides and the flow of the Solway.

The Solway Firth has been the scene of many drowning fatalities in the past, but a shocking tragedy occurred in its waters in March 1935, when three young men working on the demolition of the viaduct were swept to their deaths by the treacherous tidal current. The victims of the sad affair were Mr William Adam from Edinburgh who acted as Clerk of Works for the LMS Railway Company, Mr William Morgan from Barrhead who was a foreman engineer, and Mr George Walker, a labourer from Annan.

The men were engaged in the removal of the huge cast iron piles which formed the foundation of the structure. Formerly the piles were removed by a dredger fitted with a steam winch, but this method was discontinued in favour of a steam crane placed on the bridge itself. The men used a rowing boat to fix the hawser of the crane to the head of each piles prior to its being hauled aloft. Mr Samuel Rae of Back-of-the-Hill Annan had been engaged by the contractors as boatman and he took charge of the boat while the other men attended to the piles. The day before the tragedy Mr Rae had met with an accident, as a result of which he sustained a badly lacerated hand and was unable to resume duty the next day.

None of the victims of the tragedy had much knowledge of the management of a boat, nor were they acquainted with the tremendous speed and dangerous cross-currents of the Solway tide, and it was wholly due to their ignorance of these matters that they lost their lives.

The accident happened about 11.10 am when the three men were in a boat at the furthermost end of the existing structure (which was about half a mile from shore) attending to the removal of the piles, the boat being moored to the viaduct by means of a rope. At this particular time the flood tide had been running for some hours, and aided by an exceptionally strong south-west wind the tidal waters simply roared up the Firth.

Suddenly the mooring rope, which held the boat to the bridge, broke, and before the men could do anything the fierce current swept them away. The men had only one oar between them and with this they tried to make for the shore, only half a mile away, but the strength of the tide and the roughness of the waters rendered their task quite impossible, and the men had simply to drift wherever the current carried them. The tide swept the men towards the fishermen's poke nets; they managed to clear the first set of nets and made a desperate struggle to avoid the second set, but the current was too strong for them and they crashed into the nets broadside on and became half submerged. Some of the workers ran from the viaduct along the shore in an effort to reach another rowing boat which was moored at about the low water mark, but the tide was coming in with such speed that their effort were unavailing, and they could only look on as their comrades fought in vain for life. All three victims of the shocking tragedy wore high rubber leggings and were non-swimmers and had no chance of saving themselves when the boat capsized.

Next day, the body of William Adam was discovered at the Loch Fisheries, almost totally buried in the sand. The body of William Morgan was found the day after in the same location as Adam's body, again almost totally buried in the sand. The body of George Walker was never found.

Mr A. Cain of Annan, the crane driver, said that if the rope had held for another few minutes the tragedy would not have happened, as he was just preparing to lower the hawser to lift the boat and the men on to the bridge, which he did at the end of each day's work.

The dismantling of the viaduct took 19 months to complete, and in November 1935 what had been the longest viaduct in Great Britain (until the Tay Bridge was built) was reduced to a few bits and pieces of scrap iron sticking out of the Solway bed. The schooner *General Havelock* which had been used in the dismantling was sold at Annan for breaking up for firewood for just £5.

Chapter Six

The Last Years of the Railway

With the formation of the LMS in 1923 the line was divided, and that part south of the Bowness end of the viaduct went to the North Western Division and all north of this to the Northern Division. Annan (SJR) became Annan Shawhill from 2nd June, 1924. The part of the line between Bowness and Kirkbride Junction lay disused until sold with the bridge. The part from Abbey Junction to Brayton continued to be worked by the Maryport and Carlisle Section until 14th February, 1933, when traffic using this line stopped. Track lifting of this section took place in 1937. In 1927 the former Caledonian Shed and turntable at Brayton were removed and the siding junctions rearranged for storage of surplus wagons.

On the Northern Section, passenger traffic was withdrawn from 27th April, 1931 as between Kirtlebridge and Annan Shawhill but goods trains continued to run twice weekly until the outbreak of the 1939 war and then finished until an airfield was made, when the short portion from Kirtlebridge came back into use. There is some ambiguity about what happened between 1941 and 1947, but in 1947 there was no track north of the Annan goods shed for at least 2 miles. Most of the line to Kirtlebridge was lifted with the closure of the airfield. In 1953 the portion from Annan Goods to the junction with the loop from the G&SW line was closed and in January 1955, this part, the loop on the exchange line and more than half of the Solway Junction extension towards the bridge site were removed. The exchange loop was retained as a refuge siding for a further 10 years or so.

Today some reminders of the Solway Junction Railway still remain. The embankments are there; on the English side sandstone blocks have fallen away to expose rusting steel pillars looking for all the world like columns marking the site of some ancient Greek settlement. On the Scottish side, the embankment is in a far better state of repair, for it carries the large sewage pipes taking the effluent from the nuclear power station at Chapelcross to the sea.

KIRTLEBRIDGE AND ANNAN.

The Passenger Train Service between Kirtlebridge and Annan (Shawhill) has been discontinued.

The Omnibus Services operated by the Caledonian Omnibus Company between Lockerbie and Annan will make contact with Kirtlebridge Station.

Extract from Bradshaw's Timetable, 1931.

North British Railway Company. ___

CHIEF GOODS MANAGER'S OFFICE.

GLASGOW, 26th January, 1917.

Circular No. L. 332/2,104 A.

To Agents and others concerned.

CLOSING OF CERTAIN GOODS STATIONS AND SIDINGS ON CALEDONIAN RAILWAY.

With reference to my Circular L. 332/2,104 of 8th January, 1917 ; please note that, until further notice, the Solway Branch of the Caledonian Railway will be closed from 1st proximo, and traffic of all descriptions for their Stations at

Bowness,   Abbey Junction,   Whitrigg,   Bromfield,   Brayton,

must not be accepted for conveyance unless it will arrive at destination prior to 31st instant.

The closing of the Branch will preclude traffic from being exchanged at Abbey or Kirkbride Junctions as heretofore, and the following amended instructions as to Routing must be given effect to in respect of traffic which cannot be exchanged at these points prior to 31st current :—

Traffic with	Routes by which Traffic must be Invoiced and Wagons Labelled.
Caledonian Company's Stations for which the route at present is *via* Abbey Holme or *via* Kirkbride,	*Via* Carlisle and Cal. Rly.
Cleator and Workington Junction Company's Stations.	
Cockermouth, Keswick, and Penrith Company's Stations at Bassenthwaite. Embleton. Braithwaite. Keswick.	
Furness Company's Stations at Bootle. St. Bees. Drigg. Seascale. Netherton. Silecroft. Ravinglass.	*Via* CARLISLE
London & North-Western Company's Stations at Branthwaite. Flimby. Woodend. Beckermet. Frizington. Whitehaven. Bridgefoot. Harrington. Winder. Cleator Moor. Moor Row. Wrightgreen. Crossfield. Parton. Workington. Distington. Rowrah. Workington Bridge. Eskett. Sellafield. Yeathouse. Egremont. Ullock.	and M. & C. RLY.
Maryport and Carlisle Company's Stations.	

CLOSING OF ROSSLYNLEE STATION (NORTH BRITISH).

The arrangement notified in Circular L. 332/2,104 of 8th instant providing for traffic in full wagon loads being dealt with at Rosslynlee as a Siding under charge of Rosslyn Castle Station has been amended to include Live Stock and such goods traffic as was dealt with prior to the closing of Rosslynlee Passenger Station.

Please note and acknowledge receipt.

W. ANDREW,
Chief Goods Manager.

Notice of closure of stations in 1917 on the Solway Junction Railway.

NORTH BRITISH RAILWAY COMPANY.

Chief Goods Manager's Office,
Circular No. G.3583.   GLASGOW, 31st August, 1921.

TO AGENTS AND OTHERS CONCERNED.

CLOSING OF SOLWAY BRANCH OF THE CALEDONIAN RAILWAY.

The Caledonian Company intimate that the Solway Branch of their line will be closed entirely on and after 1st proximo, and that they will accordingly cease to deal with traffic at the following Stations and Sidings:-

> Bowness.
> Whitrigg.
> Abbey Junction.
>   Kirkbride Moss Litter Company's Siding.
> Bromfield.
>   Fielding & Company's Siding.
> Brayton.
>   Brayton No.4 Colliery.

Traffic must not, therefore, be accepted for delivery by the Caledonian Company at these places.

It should, of course, be kept in view that the Kirkbride Moss Litter Co's Siding, is connected with this Company's system at Kirkbride Station, and that the Maryport & Carlisle Company have a Station at Brayton and have also connection with Brayton No.4 Colliery.

All rates in operation with Bowness, Whitrigg, Abbey Junction, Bromfield, and Brayton, Caledonian Railway, fall to be cancelled.

In view of the permanent closure of the Solway Branch, the instructions in Cir. G.3563 of 5th July,1921, respecting the routing of traffic for certain Stations via "CARLISLE and M.& C.RLY" instead of "Carlisle N.B. Abbey and Brayton", will continue in operation.

Please note, advise all concerned and acknowledge receipt on annexed form.

                    JOHN.C.CHRISTIE,
                    Chief Goods Manager.

ACKNOWLEDGMENT FORM.

To be detached and returned by first train after receipt.

I beg to acknowledge receipt of Circular No.G.3583 of 31st August,1921, regarding "CLOSING OF SOLWAY BRANCH OF THE CALEDONIAN RAILWAY", to which I will attend specially.

To   Signature....................
    John.C.Christie,Esq.,   Station.....................
    Chief Goods Manager,   Date....................192
    GLASGOW.   Per

Closure Notice for the Branch issued August 1921.
Courtesy Scottish Record Office, Ref: BR/NBR/4/220

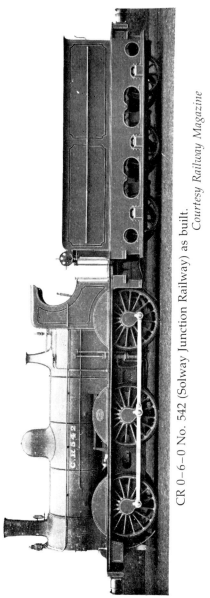

CR 0–6–0 No. 542 (Solway Junction Railway) as built.
Courtesy Railway Magazine

Solway Junction Railway 0–4–2 WT No. 1 (CR No. 540) as built.
Courtesy Railway Magazine

Chapter Seven

The Locomotives of the Solway Junction Railway

When the Solway Junction Railway ordered its first engines, Neilson & Co. had in stock four locomotives which suited its requirements. These four engines had been built in 1866 for the Northampton & Banbury Railway Co., but had been left on the builder's hands due to the Banbury company's financial difficulties.

These four engines were delivered in 1868 along with two new 0–6–0 engines ordered for the mineral trains. The two engines which took the SJR numbers 1 and 2 were 0–4–2 type well tanks with weatherboards only. They needed canopies over the footplate shortly after going into service because of the exposed nature of the line. They had inside cylinders of 16 in. diameter by 20 in. stroke. The coupled wheels were 5 ft 6 in. in diameter and the wheelbase was 17 ft. The capacity of the well tank was 450 gallons, while the capacity of the coal bunker was 25 cwt. The length over the buffers was 30 ft 1 in. The working pressure of 130 lb. and the heating surface was 924.5 sq.ft of tubes and 84.7 sq.ft of firebox, making a total of 1,009.2 sq.ft. The total weight on the axles in working order was 36 tons 2 cwt. 2 qrs.

The CR Nos. were 540 and 541 (maker's numbers 1217 and 1218 of 1866). Both engines were put on the duplicate list as 540A and 541A in 1892. In 1899 they became Nos. 1354 and 1355 respectively. No. 540 was withdrawn in 1900, while the remaining engine became 1541 in 1901. It was, however, withdrawn in the same year.

SJR Nos. 3 and 4 were 0–4–2 type tender engines with cylinders, motion, wheels and boilers interchangeable with well tanks Nos. 1 and 2. The tenders ran on four wheels and had a wheelbase of 8 ft 10 in. Their capacities were 2½ tons of coal and 1,700 gallons of water. The length of the engine and tender over the buffers was 42 ft 1½ in., and total wheelbase was 30 ft 8 in. The engine wheelbase was 14 ft 6 in., the total weight on the axles in working order was 28 tons 13 cwt; the tender weighed 20 tons 1 cwt.

The CR Nos. when received were 452 and 453 (maker's numbers 1219 and 1220 of 1866), and in 1877 they were renumbered 322 and 323. In 1887 they became 322A and 323A. The first one received number 1279 when withdrawn in 1899. The second one became 1280 in 1899 and 1323 in 1900, being withdrawn in 1906.

SJR Nos. 5 and 6 were 0–6–0 type tender engines ordered in 1868 by mutual agreement with the CR Co. They never bore SJ Nos., being

CR 0–4–2 No. 1323 (original Solway Junction Railway No. 4).
Courtesy Railway Magazine

Solway Junction Railway 0–4–2 (CR Nos. 452 and 453) as built.
Courtesy Railway Magazine

given CR Nos. 542 and 543 when built by Neilson & Co. The cylinders were inside and were of 17 in. diameter by 24 in. stroke. The driving wheels were 5 ft 1¾ in. diameter and the engine wheelbase 15 ft. The axles were of Yorkshire iron and the tyres of Krupps cast steel. Only one injector was provided. The heating surface was: 176 brass tubes 2 in. in diameter, 957.05 sq.ft; firebox 86.95 sq.ft; total 1,044 sq.ft. The grate area was 16.58 sq.ft and working pressure 130 lb. per sq.in. The boiler was 4 ft 1 in. in diameter outside at the front (and smallest) ring. The distance between tubeplates was 10 ft 4⅝in.

The total weight on the axles was 34 tons; the tender ran on six wheels of 3 ft 9 in. diameter spaced at 5 ft 8¾in. centres, making a total tender wheelbase of 11 ft 5½in. The total wheel base of engine and tender was 34 ft 10 in. and the length of the engine over buffers was 47 ft. The tender carried 1,800 gallons of water and 4 tons of coal and weighed 25 tons 19 cwt. 2 qrs in working order. The axles were of Yorkshire iron and the tyres of cast steel. The weight of the engine and tender empty was 30 tons 17 cwt., and 13 tons 17 cwt. 2 qrs respectively.

The CR numbers were 542 and 543 (Neilson & Co. 1388 and 1389 of 1868) which they carried until 1892, when they became Nos. 542A and 543A.

As these engines were beginning to wear out McIntosh considered replacing them, but the cost was considered to be too great and the engines were sent to St Rollox to be reboilered with standard boilers as fitted to the 0–6–0 side tanks. These boilers had a heating surface of 1,086 sq.ft, of which the firebox produced 111 sq.ft and the tubes 975 sq.ft. The grate area was 17 sq.ft and the working pressure 150 lb. The weight was scarcely altered. After the reboilering, which was done in March 1898 (No. 542) and November 1897 (No. 543) respectively, the engines returned to their old job. In 1897 both had been taken from the duplicate list and numbered 381 and 382 respectively. No. 381 was brought in for rebuilding in March 1902, and No. 382 followed in February 1903. Some time subsequent to this both engines received other tenders to replace their own, which had worn out. No. 382 obtained a rebuilt passenger one with a footboard for the shunter added, whereas No. 381 acquired a four-wheeled one adapted for passenger working and also provided with a footboard for the shunter. No. 382 had to have its leading and trailing wheels replaced with cast iron wheels fitted with steel tyres after a mishap in 1920, details of which are unknown.

Both of the 0–6–0 type engines lasted to become LMS stock in 1923 with the numbers 17101 and 17102 respectively. They continued to work on the now shortened SJ section between Annan and Kirtle-

CR 0–4–2WT No. 540A (ex-Solway Junction Railway) as finally running.
Courtesy Railway Magazine

CR 0–6–0ST No. 539.   *Courtesy Railway Magazine*

bridge until withdrawn in 1927 and 1928 respectively. These were the oldest CR engines to have LMS numbers.

After working on the SJ section for some years the 0–4–2 well tanks were sent to Glasgow (South Side sheds) to work on the Rutherglen to London Road section, then for a short period worked on the Dundee to Abroath Joint line. Both returned to Glasgow. No. 540 went on to Perth and shortly afterwards was sent to work the Millisle Branch (about 1890) and finished its days there.

No. 541 went to Grangemouth for the Larbert & Grahamston trains, and finally finished up at Perth as the Methven branch engine. The 0–4–2 tender engines were taken from the Solway Junction section when the ore traffic began to decline rapidly, and worked between Carstairs, Lanark and Muirkirk. Later one went to Lockerbie and the other to the Brechin to Bridge of Dun section.

Engine No. 7 of the Solway Junction Railway was destined to appear more than once in the Railway stock list. It was an 0–6–0 type saddle tank of Manning Wardle's standard design, having the maker's number of 196 of 1866. It was supplied new to Eckersley & Bayliss at Chesterfield, but in the following year was sold to Brasswy & Co., who were the contractors for the Solway Junction Railway. It had inside cylinders 11 in. in diameter by 16 in. stroke, and coupled wheels of 3 ft diameter. After completion of the line the SJR took over the engine, as they expected to have a use for it as the yard shunting engine. On coming to the Caledonian Railway it was given number 539. In January 1872, it was disposed of to the contractors for the Wigtownshire Railway.

The sheds of the Solway Junction Railway were based at Kirtlebridge and Brayton. The shed at Kirtlebridge was opened in September 1869, and was a two-road building for four locomotives. It was demolished under a local order on 16th July, 1895, being replaced by a two-road shed of wooden cladding on a timber frame, estimated to cost £230. A 42 ft turntable had been in use since 1869 but coaling was carried out from open wagons stabled on an adjacent siding. McIntosh on 10th May, 1904 recommended 'that the locomotive coal siding be slewed nearer the siding in which the engines stand while being coaled' at a cost of £20. Early on, the locomotive water supply had been arranged with 'John Irving of Burnfoot and others to be taken from a pond on the Estate of Braes' at £8 per annum. It was piped to a single column on the turntable road, and was the only water available at Kirtlebridge.

This new shed could comfortably house two locomotives, though at times more may have been allocated. By 1914 there were two 'old Oban bogies' allocated at Carlisle, with one in use 'fortnight about' for the Solway Junction Rly workings. They replaced the 0–4–2s on the passenger workings but goods had, since 1869, been given over to the Solway Junction Railway 0–6–0s of 1868. These survived into the late 'twenties as LMS Nos. 17101 and 17102, the only 0–6–0s permitted to cross the Solway Viaduct. Kirtlebridge shed had been a sub-shed of Carlisle since opening in 1869 but did not survive the LMS Depression stratagem, closing on 25th April, 1931 when the truncated line to Annan was finally closed to passenger traffic.

The shed at Brayton (opposite the 21 mile post) was a little shed based some yards east of Brayton station, and was used by both the Solway Junction Railway and the Maryport to Carlisle Railway. It was a two-road shed, barely able to accommodate a pair of 0–6–0s. Both roads continued through the shed, one of them on to a 42 ft turntable; a well sunk nearby supplied a tank and column on the turntable approach.

The shed itself reportedly came into use on 13th September, 1869 but was abandoned in 1895/1896. It was demolished around 1904, leaving only the turntable in place; this was still in position in 1923, but engines continued to stable overnight until at least 1909 and probably to 1921, when the viaduct closed.

Table 1

The Locomotives of The Solway Junction Railway

CR No.	Maker	Date	Type	Maker's No.	Renumbered	With-drawn
540	Neilson	1866	0–4–2WT	1217	540A in 1892, 1354 in 1899	1900
541	Neilson	1866	0–4–2WT	1218	541A in 1892, 1355 in 1899, 1541 in 1901	1901
452	Neilson	1866	0–4–2	1219	322 in 1877, 322A in 1887, 1279 in 1899	1899
453	Neilson	1866	0–4–2	1220	323 in 1877, 323A in 1887, 1280 in 1899, 1323 in 1900	1906
542	Neilson	1868	0–6–0	1388	542A in 1892, 381 in 1897, 17101 in 1923	1927
543	Neilson	1868	0–6–0	1389	543A in 1892, 382 in 1897, 17102 in 1923	1928
539	Manning Wardle	1866	0–6–0ST	196·		1882

Chapter Eight
The Route Described

At Kirtlebridge (the northern starting point of the line) the SJR joined at a junction with the Caledonian Railway facing towards Glasgow, together with freight sidings and a small engine shed. Leaving Kirtlebridge, the single line of the Solway Junction route bore rapidly away to the south on gradients of considerable severity.

The line soon transversed a deep cutting, where a large stone quarry was located, whose traffic was provided with a loading bank alongside the line. The station at Annan (Shawhill) was reached some 5½ miles from Kirtlebridge; this station was on the outskirts of the town and had a single platform, but there was provision for a second platform if it had been necessary.

Leaving Annan station, a deep cutting was traversed, beyond which the line crossed over the main line of the former Glasgow & South Western Railway by means of an iron girder bridge. Immediately beyond the bridge was a junction for the spur line (32 chains in length) which ended in a double junction with the main line of the GSW section. At its west end this spur line was controlled by a Solway Junction Box, Annan station (main) being a quarter of a mile further on.

Continuing the journey from the point of the junction with the Annan spur line, the railway ran on a steep embankment, which had a descent of about 1 in 80 to the Solway Viaduct. After crossing the viaduct the railway ran on top of an embankment until it reached Bowness station, which had two platforms and sidings.

Leaving Bowness, the line rose steadily, passing through pleasant countryside, then through a small wood until, three miles from Bowness, it reached the single line station of Whitrigg, which had a single siding behind the platform and a covered waiting room. Immediately south of the station was a level crossing operated from a ground frame on the platform.

The line made its way across sandy soil until after half a mile the line crossed the River Wampool by an iron bridge, which was of a similar design to the viaduct. The line was now passing through rather flat agricultural land which was prone to flooding. The line then went on to a junction with the North British Silloth to Carlisle line at Kirkbride Junction, which was some distance from the North British Kirkbride station. The line ran along the NB's Silloth branch until it reached Abbey Junction where both the NB and the SJR maintained stations for interchange purposes, these stations being some distance apart.

At Abbey Junction there was a crossover to the Solway Junction siding which had a dead end, followed by a NB loop with a platform on each side. Leaving Abbey Junction, the line was back on the metals of the Solway Junction Railway; it soon reached the station of Bromfield, which had a single platform and a small goods yard.

After leaving Bromfield the line rose sharply for the last 1¾ miles to the final station at Brayton some 21 miles from Kirtlebridge; here on the north side were extensive Solway Junction sidings. On the other side of the station was a through loop where shunting could be carried out.

Table Two
Point to Point Distances

	miles	chains
Kirtlebridge	0	0
Annan (Shawhill)	5	35
Shawhill Jn	5	79
(Shawhill Jn to GSW Jn 32 chains)		
Bowness-on-Solway	8	10
Whitrigg	11	03
Kirkbride Jn	12	13
Abbey Jn	15	75
Bromfield	19	10
Brayton Jn	21	03
Brayton	21	18

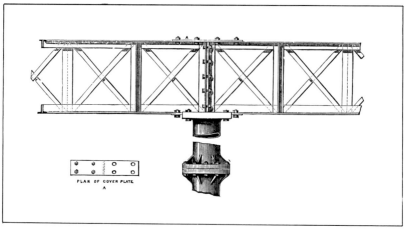

Detail of girders on the Solway Viaduct.   *Courtesy, The Engineer*

Appendix One

Chronology

First sod on the Railway cut: 28th March, 1865.

Formal completion of work: 27th June, 1868.

Open for Freight traffic: 13th September, 1869.

First Passenger train: 8th August, 1870.

Last train across the viaduct: 31st August, 1921.

Viaduct demolished: 1934–35.

Remains: embankments; Bowness station, Brayton station, Annan Shawhill station and Bromfield station houses are now dwellings.

Appendix Two

Correspondence concerning the Building of the Solway Viaduct

(Copies of letters written by George Potter Esq., to Messrs Waring Brothers and Eckersley. All letters were addressed to Mr W. Eckersley.)

19th April, 1865

Dear Mr Eckersley,

I have let the staging of the wharf to Holden at 6*d.* per cubic foot, to include piles, bracings, flooring complete. The staging for the viaduct is to be an after arrangement depending upon the manner in which the viaduct contract is let. Holden is anxious to take the timber and iron work, and he says he can find men experienced in screw driving, but altho' it would be no harm having a tender from him, I don't think it would do to let to him.

2nd May, 1865

I intend letting Holden go on with the staging for the viaduct when he has finished the wharf. The capstan bars are here but they will require altering to fit these piles. I had a man today to look at the specifications and plan, he is going to give a tender for the erection.

5th June, 1865

I see under the head of guarantee and liability on the specifications that we are to guarantee the stability of the works, and take all the risks of accidents to the viaduct and Solway banks, and I think you ought to bring this clause to the attention of Mr Waring. It is an objectionable clause I see in the specification, and as there was no Solway viaduct in the contract, I do not think we ought to guarantee that work after it was once certified for especially at the point, we have to maintain. I should not hurry over the contract, and I should find some way to put off signing it.

10th August, 1865

North has not yet got his screwing machine to work, it is to be ready tomorrow. I shall believe it when I see it at work.

12th August, 1865

I am going to Glasgow on Tuesday to take delivery of the steamer. If in the meantime I do not hear from you, I will see you down here on Monday or Tuesday.

27th February, 1866

It has become quite evident that we cannot drive 216 piles in the Solway where we are driving now at 15 feet, they go very stiff, scarcely an inch in 6 blows, but as the ground is uncertain, it is impossible to say before hand how the piles in the same pier will go after driving one pile, for instance in the 139th pier from Seafield the most westerly pile down 13 ft 6 in. at the rate of ¾" to a blow. The two next westernly in same pier would not go down below 12 feet at that rate, those which remain take from 6 to 12 blows to get them down an inch.

We can of course cut the top of these piles for the remainder of the pier, but after all, this is only patch work for the A pile can never be so solid as the original casting, for you can never be sure that a short pile has gone down to a good bottom. After consulting with Mr North in the matter, we have both arrived at the conclusion that best and surest plan to make a good job is that all the A piles should be cast 20 feet in length, also be in low as the pile will go with a 20 cwt. monkey and a four foot fall and effect of ½" at a blow which ought to be quite when to stop driving. And that A piles should be cast 15 feet in length and be drawn to the datum of 87–57, the outside rakers would all be in line.

The four intermediate would be down to solid bottom and the B, would still be making up lengths.

The walings would be placed at 87–50 as now extended. I have spoken to Mr Kerrow on the subject and he very much approves the idea, and is going to write to Mr Brunlees on the subject just stated, I think it will be a considerable help to us in forwarding the work, and there is no doubt that it will make a much better job for the company, if you understand my explanation – have the kindness to see Mr Brunlees and get his consent if possible. There is no time to be lost, as we must order A piles at once.

6th June, 1866

I visited Falkirk yesterday and arranged with them to cast the following daily.

        10 – A piles
         5 – A2 "
         6 – B   "
         2 – B2 "
        ─────────
        23 piles daily

This I hope will keep us going, it is a rate which is the limit of production at Falkirk.

12th November, 1866

We had a serious accident at the south side on Saturday morning, the middle bearer of the riveting platform broke, a man and a boy who were on it at the time fell on the scaur below. The man was killed and the boy received concussion of the brain, he is going favourably.

I have just returned from the inquest, the jury returned a verdict of accidental death.

Abbey Junction, looking north.   *Courtesy Railway Magazine*

Index